UNCLE FRED'S
HISTORY O
WESTCLIFF

Steve Crancher

Ian Henry Publications

ISBN 0 86025 478 X

Printed by Esparto Digital, Ltd.
Slack Lane, Derby DE22 3DS
for
Ian Henry Publications, Ltd.
20 Park Drive, Romford, Essex RM1 4LH

ACKNOWLEDGEMENTS

I wish to thank the following who helped with information for this book -

Miss Ridd
Stan
Essex Record Office

This book is dedicated to Miss Ridd

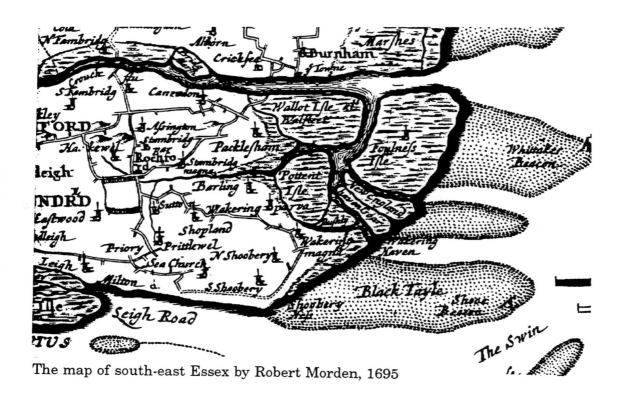

The map of south-east Essex by Robert Morden, 1695

I

The wind howled and the rain hammered relentlessly at the sodden ground. All around me, trees heaved and creaked eerily. A flash of lightning briefly lit my way and this was soon followed by a great clap of thunder. I trudged on wearily, soaked, my umbrella having been made useless by the cruel wind. At last, to my relief, I heard a gate rattling in its catch and saw a glimmer of light in a tiny window. This was it; Uncle Fred's cottage. If it had a thatched roof, whitewashed external walls, diamond lead-lights and a picket fence, I didn't see. But I did see that, inside, the fire glowed and crackled invitingly.

I don't have the faintest idea why my thoughts wandered in this way as I pulled up, in my warm Mini Metro, outside the block of flats in which Uncle Fred lives. The terrible storm was a slight drizzle beneath a grey sky; the garden gate a security entry system; and the crackling fire an invisible radiator. But Uncle Fred was just the same, and perhaps he really should live in an isolated, low-beamed cottage. But this is the 1990s and romance and eccentricity have become things of the past - or so the pessimists like to think.

Uncle Fred is very forgetful, and yet he has an excellent memory. He is more than eighty years of age, and probably less than one hundred, but I can't be any more specific. His hair is white. Some might say it's grey but I once saw him in a clean vest and it was a perfect match. He makes excellent tea and, occasionally, smokes a pipe, and in consequence of these facts his apartment has a rather pleasant aroma somewhere between the two.

As we sat in our armchairs, each holding a cup of hot, dark-brown liquid that is generally known merely as tea, but at Uncle Fred's is called either `lovely tea' or `excellent tea', he suggested that I ought to be doing something more worthwhile with my Saturday afternoons. The football season was over for another year, so a visit to Roots Hall was not an option. Perhaps the High Street to do some shopping or watch a film at the cinema; I mentioned a new film that I particularly wanted to see.

"New?" said Uncle Fred. "That isn't a new film - must be a remake. I took your Aunt Sissy to see that film at the Mascot, back in the thirties."

"The Mascot?" I inquired. "Where's that?"

"You mean to say you haven't heard of it?" he said, surprised. "It was on the corner of Beedell Avenue and London Road. Look; there's a picture of it."

I turned and looked at his print of the Mascot Cinema but my memory was unjogged.

"Burnt down back in 1964," he informed me. "Well, truth be told, it was gutted and demolished later. They say it was started by some kids throwing fireworks around, and one of these didn't go off but lay smouldering by the screen; nobody noticed, and they locked up and went home for the night. The fire was spotted by a chap just before midnight and before long a crowd had gathered to watch the firemen at work. One enterprising chap, who owned a coffee bar nearby, opened up and made a fortune. And I'm not kidding - the films due to be shown that week were *Ursus in the Land of Fire* and *Gunsmoke*."

"Really?" I said, and almost added, `you're kidding' before remembering that he'd claimed he wasn't.

"Yes, Sissy and I visited the old Mascot many a time. It was quite a posh old place; there was a fishpond in the foyer. Sometimes

The Palace Theatre, 1918. Showing is *Little Miss Llewelyn*

we'd just go and sit in the café for a cup of tea. In fact I proposed to Sissy in the Mascot café; got down on my knee in front of everyone and Sissy blushed, but she accepted all the same and everyone smiled. People didn't applaud things like that in those days; they just smiled."

"That's lovely, Uncle Fred," I said. "I didn't know that. You must have been sad to see it burn down."

"Yes, I suppose I was really. I used to go there as a kid when it was called the Leigh Road Theatre, when the London Road was called Leigh Road. I remember once in about 1929 a charabanc went out of control and crashed into it. It didn't cause too much damage though; I think it smashed a billboard. Also I used to go to the King's Cinema. I suppose you've never heard of that either."

"Well, no, Uncle. To be honest, I haven't."

"Well then," said Uncle Fred. "The King's - or the King's Hall as it was originally called - was behind the shops in Hamlet Court Road where the car park is now. Obviously it's long gone but the arcade is still there."

"Ah. Is that about three or four shops down on the right?" I asked. "Tiled floor with an archway?"

"That's the place," said Uncle Fred.

"I've often wondered why that was there. It seemed to be such an extravagant entrance to a car park."

"Well that's the reason," he said. "And if you want to know, it opened in 1907 and in 1940 it was converted into a dance hall for the troops for the duration of the war. Did I tell you when The Mascot opened?"

"No, Uncle Fred; you didn't."

"It was in 1912, the same year as the Palace Theatre."

"I know where that is," I said, with a smile.

Hamlet Court Road, 1905

"But did you know that they showed movies there between 1930 and 1932?"

"No, I didn't."

"Then came the Metropole which opened in 1939. Before you ask, you'll know where it is when I tell you that in 1954 it became the Essoldo, in 1972 the Classic, and then finally, the Cannon. Of course, even that's gone now."

"It's amazing, isn't it," I reflected. "You don't think of Westcliff having any history, but I suppose all that is now history."

"No history?" said Uncle Fred, somewhat emphatically. "Westcliff has plenty of history."

"Has it?"

"Well now, let me ask you a question. Have you heard of a place called Milton Hamlet?"

"No. Never heard of it."

"That's why you don't think Westcliff has a history. Not so long ago Westcliff-on-Sea was Milton Hamlet."

"So that's why there's Milton Road and Hamlet Court Road," I said, thinking I was displaying astute powers of deduction although I realise, retrospectively, that it didn't really take too much working out.

"That's right," said Uncle Fred. "Milton Hamlet was within the parish of Prittlewell. But before that it was known as Middleton - meaning the 'middle town' between Leigh and Southchurch - and, before that, Mildentuna. Also just plain Milton, because it might not have always been a hamlet. There's a story that older people of the early 1800s could remember seeing the foundations of a church at low tide. This church is said to have been engulfed by the sea sometime between the twelfth and fourteenth centuries."

I'm interested in history so, having discovered that my home town is older than the ninety or so years I had always thought it to

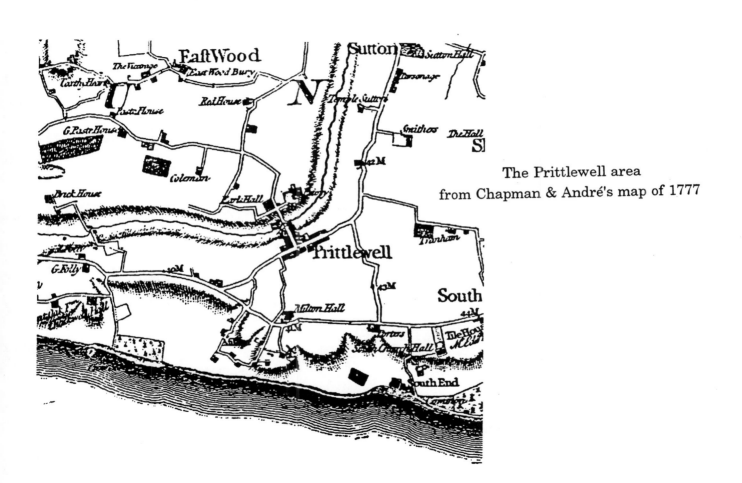

The Prittlewell area
from Chapman & André's map of 1777

be, I asked Uncle Fred to tell me more.

"In Saxon times," he began, "Milton was royal property, and in the year 824 AD it was given to the monks of Christchurch in Canterbury. The Domesday Book mentioned Milton as having eight villeins, fifteen borders, eight ploughs and a serf."

"Eight villains?"

"Villagers. Villeins is the old word for it. Borders were smallholders, ploughs were ploughs, and the serf had nothing to do with riding waves."

I grinned at his joke. "So all this was in 1086?" I said, trying to show my knowledge of history, limited though it is.

"Very good," said Uncle Fred. "Or thereabouts. Then, sometime between 1162 and 1170, Thomas-à-Becket, the Archbishop of Canterbury, confirmed the tithes of the township of Milton and all the parochial rights to the priory at Prittlewell. It's my guess that this is soon after they lost the church.

"These monks owned a place called Milton Hall, which they leased out. There's a picture of it from about 1890. It was broken into in 1381 by the villagers who'd joined the Peasants' Revolt. They burned all the records in the hope of gaining freedom from the Lord of the Manor but, unfortunately for them, when the revolt was over they had to pay to be re-admitted to their holdings. Milton reverted to the Crown in 1539 when the monasteries were dissolved."

"By Henry the Eighth," I interposed.

"Quite right. Milton Hall was then granted to Sir Richard Rich of Rochford Hall, and his heirs. These heirs were the Earls of Warwick and in the late seventeenth century the hall was purchased from them by Daniel Scratton of Prittlewell Priory. In the 1820s a descendant of his, John Bone Scratton - a very strange middle

Nazareth House   Reproduced with the permission of Essex County Libraries

name I know - rebuilt the place and laid out the grounds.

"In the nineteenth century it was bought by one Reverend J. Wonnacott, for use as a boarding school. In 1880 he sold it on to the Sisters of Nazareth, who used it as a convent and home for the aged infirm and destitute children. By 1882 it'd been renamed Nazareth House."

"Yeh, I know where that is," I said.

"Well, this order still owns it. One more thing I know about the place is that, in 1826, a forty-seven foot whale died after being stranded on the beach at Leigh. It was taken to the grounds of a public house in Southend and put on show at a penny a look. There were many customers, because Southend was a fairly popular seaside resort at that time. Of course, as days went by, the flesh rotted and the stink kept people away, and eventually the bones

were moved to and kept on the grounds of Milton Hall.

"And that brings to an end my history of Milton Hall, cum Nazareth House. If you look at those two maps on the wall, you'll see it. The first is from 1777, the second from about 1873."

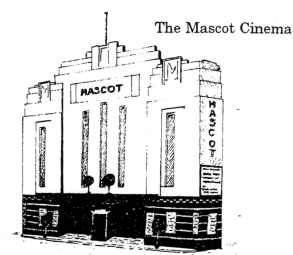

The Mascot Cinema

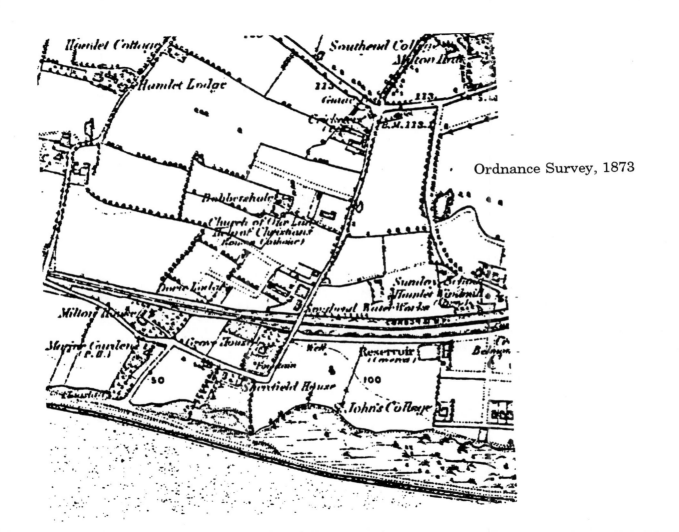

Ordnance Survey, 1873

II

Of course, when I looked at the maps I didn't stop at Milton Hall. The more detailed of them, from 1873, drew my attention to other places.

"Hamlet Windmill," I said in surprise when I saw it. "Was there really a windmill in Westcliff?"

"There was indeed," replied Uncle Fred. "At the junction of Avenue Road and Park Road, opposite the Methodist Church, which was built in 1870. Avenue Road, by the way, is one of the oldest roads in the town. I'll tell you what I know, which isn't much. A mill was built here in 1299 at a cost of fifteen pounds, five shillings and ten pence. In 1848 it was occupied by Lazarus and Company, and in 1869 it was owned by another Daniel Scratton and leased to a John Lacell. Unfortunately for John Lacell, Scratton wanted to sell it so he gave him his notice and sold it, with a five-bedroom house, for £1,000 to Thomas Arnold, who was still living there in 1874. It was demolished in 1892 as Southend grew.

In the year 1400, John Holland, the Duke of Exeter, was involved in an unsuccessful rebellion against Henry the fourth. He made his escape to Essex and there, possibly at Tilbury, got aboard an outgoing ship, but this was driven back by contrary winds. Back onshore he was arrested by the people of Milton, at the windmill. He to was taken from there to Pleshey and subsequently beheaded."

"Poor chap," I commented. "Lost his head because of contrary winds."

"That's it as far as the windmill's concerned, but I can tell you about others making their escape this way."

"Please do," I said.

"Very well. One of the martyrs during the

12

Hamlet Mill   Reproduced with the permission of Southend Museums Service

Reformation was named John Frith. His adherence to the doctrines of Luther led to his being imprisoned, with others, in an underground cave somewhere in Cambridge. Frith escaped and tried to get to the continent. At this time Milton was a port and it was here that he was arrested. He was taken away, tried, and burned at the stake at Smithfield in London in 1534."

"Poor bloke," I said. "Lost his life because of contrary opinions."

Uncle Fred laughed before continuing, "In the reign of Bloody Mary between 1553 and 1558, a Doctor Edwin Sands, being a Protestant under a Catholic queen, escaped down the Thames from London as far as Milton where he hid himself away in the house of a man called Mower. Word got about though, so he appealed to the people of Milton to help him escape. I don't know if you know, but Mary was a very unpopular queen. She tried to force Catholicism on to the populace and was responsible for the execution of hundreds of non-conformers. It was probably because of this that the people of Milton helped Sands in his escape to Flanders. But before leaving he said to Mower's wife - who'd been married eight years and was still childless - 'Don't worry. Before one year has passed, God will give you a son,' or words to that effect. And within a year a son was born."

"Really?" I said. "Is that true?"

"Well, it's a story that's come down through the ages. I'd say it's true enough."

"So what did this Doctor Sands actually do in the first place?" I asked. "Why was he trying to escape?"

"I believe he was involved in the rising of Lady Jane Grey, which was unsuccessful. The postscript is, though, that when Mary died and good Queen Bess came to the throne, he

A Stiff Breeze, Westcliff-on-Sea

The Promenade, c.1912. Note the cycle and sidecar bottom right

returned to England and later became Archbishop of York."

"So Milton was a port, was it?"

"Yes," replied Uncle Fred. "It was mentioned as a port back in 1225, and in 1564-5 a return showed that Prittlewell had ten ships, fourteen masters and thirty-six mariners and fishermen. Seven years later, Milton Shore - as it was called - had eight ships. In 1539 men by the names of ...er...just a minute; let me think."

For a few moments he appeared to be concentrating, and then continued, "Pulter, Reed, Scott, Murdoch and Byam were quoted as being Milton mariners."

"How on earth do you remember their names?" I asked, astounded by his memory.

"In this case it's word association," he replied. "They're mariners, so I think of the word `press-gang', change it to `press-mob' and the initial letters come from that. Simple."

"It isn't simple, Uncle Fred. You've got an excellent memory."

"No I haven't," he said, dismissively. "Now then, where was I? You've put me right off. Ah, yes. One more person was arrested in Milton while trying to escape from London. His name was Anthony Tyrrell, it was 1574, and it was the opposite to Doctor Sands. Tyrrell was a Catholic under a Protestant queen. Fortunately for him, Queen Elizabeth the First was more tolerant than her step-sister Mary and he was able to make his peace with the authorities."

"And all this happened right here in Westcliff-on-Sea," I said. "The place I thought had no history."

Still standing by the map, I looked again. My route took me back to Milton Hall, and north along a country lane surrounded by open fields. I wondered if sheep or cattle might have been grazing upon them, or perhaps they were

Bridge House, 1902

freshly ploughed, or standing tall with corn. Somebody could have been working on them, harvesting the old-fashioned way, or ploughing thanks to the efforts of a large horse or two. I stopped briefly at Prittlewell, noticed, just to the left, Mill Farm, but continued northwards before stopping at a place called Bridge House.

"Mill Farm was on West Road, opposite the end of what's now Gainsborough Drive," explained Uncle Fred. "I really don't remember it, I'm afraid. I think it was demolished in the early part of this century, probably to make way for houses in Salisbury Road. I remember Bridge House though. That's it, just there."

He was pointing at another print; an attractive, if slightly square Georgian house.

"It's really nice," I said. "I suppose they demolished that as well. Where was it? Looks about the end of Fairfax Drive to me."

"That's precisely where it was," replied Uncle Fred. "Let's see now..."

He trailed off and thought for a few moments, then, with a start, continued.

"Bridge House belonged to The Drapers' Company in the second half of the nineteenth century. It was built in about 1747 but before that, in another house on the site, a man named Richard Legg lived and worked there as a tanner. That was in 1650, I believe. It was still a tan yard in 1705, but occupied by Peter Jarvis. One John Hardwick lived there in 1782. And that's about all I can remember."

"So what happened to it?" I asked.

"It was demolished in the 1960s," he replied. "I don't think it was damaged in the Meteor Incident."

"Oh good," I said. "I'd hate to think it was damaged in the Meteor Incident."

Uncle Fred had a wry grin on his old face, but said nothing.

"Come on then, Uncle Fred," I conceded. "I confess I don't have the faintest idea what you're talking about."

"Sorry, lad," he said. "One of my little games. I'll tell you about the Meteor Incident, which was a tragic accident. It was in 1951, September, I'm quite sure, because my Barbara had just started school. In this instance the meteor was an RAF jet fighter. It was doing manoeuvres over the estuary, went into a dive, and disintegrated in the air. I didn't see anything of it myself, but the pieces rained down over Westcliff. Two houses were totally destroyed, where the fuselage hit them, and a third had to be demolished later: these were in Beedell Avenue and Ramuz Drive. But another fifty or so houses in the area were damaged in one way or another. The tragedy is that four people, including the pilot - who happened to be a Leigh man - were killed."

"And all this as recently as 1951," I said. "That's terrible. I would've thought that would still be common knowledge, but it isn't."

"No, it was a long time ago. I remember a story that went round at the time. Typical British stiff-upper-lip that; finding humour in tragedy. Apparently, and this is a true story, a chap had just put on an egg to boil when it happened. He rushed out to look and heard a woman calling for help, went to her aid and found her husband had been buried under rubble. He and others who'd come to help worked with their bare hands and finally freed the poor husband, who recovered later. When the chap returned home and found that his egg was still boiling and as hard as iron."

I sort of laughed, though more out of politeness than amusement. Uncle Fred then got out of his chair and went to make another cup of tea.

The Promenade, 1925

III

As the kettle boiled in virtual silence, Uncle Fred stepped to the gap between the lounge and the kitchenette.

"Talking of boiling water, do you know anything about oysters?"

"Yes, two things," I replied. "They're shellfish and I've never eaten one."

"Well, in the eighteenth and nineteenth centuries you probably would have eaten them. Oysters were very popular at that time and this area had a thriving industry in supplying them to Londoners, being so close."

He moved forward and returned to his chair. "But oysters weren't natural to the area and the whole thing was started by chance."

"How was that then, Uncle Fred?"

"It was like this. In the year 1700 a man by the name of Joseph Outing, who was a fisherman, was returning home along the estuary after having been at sea for some time. He had some oysters on his boat that were too small to be used, so he threw them overboard somewhere near the shore. A few months later he was coming by again when he happened to see the oysters. He opened one and found that it had grown to a good size so he went down to Sussex, got some more small ones, and did the same thing again just to make sure, and the very same thing happened.

"Well, now, he must have thought to himself that there was something in this because he went to the Lord of the Manor, Daniel Scratton, leased the shore and became a very wealthy man. So if you want to be rich, that's one way to do it, although in this day and age you'd be better off throwing little cheeseburgers over."

I laughed.

"Of course, other men soon followed Mr

Swimming pool and gardens, 1935

Outing's lead, and the shoreline was divided into little oyster farms on which men could be seen raking them over at low tide."

"What," I said. "Raking the oysters?"

"That's right."

"Why?"

As I said this I heard the click of the kettle automatically switching itself off.

"Because," said Uncle Fred, "the large oysters would lay over the young ones and smother them, so they were raked to spread them out.

"The general procedure was that the oyster-men would collect the young oysters from Sussex and Dorset in February, March and April, bring them up here and leave them alone for seven or eight months, at which time they'd be ready for eating.

"One final thing on the subject is that, in January, 1826, all the oysters were killed by frost because of the shallow waters. This almost certainly happened in other years, but 1826 is the only one I can quote because I read about it in the diary of Dr Jonas Asplin."

"Who was he?"

"Simply a Prittlewell doctor who happened to keep a diary from 1826 to 1828. It's quite an interesting read, and mentions 'The Hamlet' three or four times, although nothing specially remarkable. I think the D'Aranda family lived in one of the houses there at the time."

At this point I remembered that the kettle had boiled and could see that Uncle Fred showed no sign of getting up to do anything about it. I wondered whether I ought to wait and see, or remind him, or offer to make the tea myself, but while I was thinking about it he continued his history.

"Close to the sea-front there was a pub called the Marine Gardens and I'll bet the

The Slopes, 1905

oystermen would go there after their day's work. But I don't know anything about the place, except that at some time between 1873 and 1897 it had become known as Recko House.

"Now, a little away along from this was the swimming bath. You must remember that, surely."

I did.

"Of course it was put there so that people could have a dip no matter whether the tide was in or out. It was opened in 1915 and Sissy and I, and the kids, spent many a happy hour splashing around in there.

"In 1970 it was used as a dolphinarium but then they built on it, the Westcliff Leisure Centre."

"I remember swimming there," I said. "And I'm pretty sure I saw the dolphins. And also I used to go to the disco in the leisure centre when I was a teenager. So I know it quite well down there. After the disco my friends and I would stroll, drunkenly, down to the nearest food bar and buy ourselves a greasy hamburger and chips, and smother it in watered-down tomato ketchup. Those were the days."

"How our reminiscences differ," said Uncle Fred, smiling and grimacing at the same time. "I recollect strolling - soberly - to Palmeira Arches, sitting in the shade of a parasol, and eating sausages and mash and Rossi's ice cream."

"I love Rossi's ice cream," I said, licking my lips slightly at the thought of it.

"Who doesn't?" said Uncle Fred. "You know, ex-pat Southenders who return for a nostalgic visit often buy as much as they can to take back with them to places like Canada and America."

"Really? I bet they have a fair old dry-cleaning bill when they get home," I said.

The bandstand

The Happy Valley, Southend on Sea.   Copyright.

The Happy Valley, 1908

"Would you like me to tell you about Rossi's?" asked Uncle Fred, smiling.

I nodded.

"The company was started by Pietro Rossi in the north - Consett in County Durham - and came down here in the early 1930s. The Westcliff shop was originally called the Happy Valley Café - the Happy Valley being the name given to the cliffs above it. Well, they enlarged and improved the café, and it's still being run by the Rossi family.

The Happy Valley was also the site of the first bandstand after it had been moved from the top of the cliffs. It was built in 1902, but seven years later they moved it to the Valley and built a pretty new bandstand in its place. There's a picture on the wall there of this second one. It was known as the Cakestand because of its ornate decoration, but this became structurally unsound, was demolished in 1956 and replaced by a less attractive bandstand. Then, in March, 1988, some yobboes came along on a Saturday night and burnt it down. For a time, nobody knew quite what to do with the place, but then the Council bought in an architect from Lancashire whose job it was to recreate the old cakestand. And this opened in 1990 to the sound of the Pasadena Youth Orchestra."

"I used to work there on Sundays when I was about fifteen," I recalled. "The tea was made in a huge urn; it was that instant powdered stuff with milk included in the mixture. The old folk would nag me something rotten that it tasted horrible, but it wasn't my fault."

Uncle Fred laughed. "Going back to Palmeira Arches," he said. "Did you know that they were originally built in 1905 as boat houses, or as coach houses for the hotels, but

Overcliff Hotel

West Cliff Hotel

they quickly became popular as cafés."

"No, I didn't, to be honest."

"Of course, those were the days of the hotels. There was the Palmeira Towers, the Westward Ho!, the Overcliff, the Queens and the West Cliff, to name the bigger ones. All but the West Cliff have gone now. But one thing I do remember is this: you could get a decent cup of tea in the Queens."

I wondered if all this talk of tea would remind him of the pot in the kitchenette currently awaiting the addition of boiling water. After a few moments I realised that it hadn't, so I did.

Palmeira Towers, 1910

Queens Hotel.   Westcliff-on-Sea.

Queen's Hotel, 1906

Westward Ho! Hotel, 1954

IV

Standing in his little kitchenette, Uncle Fred started chuckling to himself as he poured the freshly-boiled water into the teapot. I smiled at this, and knew that he was about to tell me more.

"Do you know," he said, walking back into the lounge holding a gingham tea-towel, "that Westcliff was nicknamed Little Jerusalem by the locals, about fifty years ago. When the train drew into the station they would announce: 'Tel Aviv!'." He chuckled again and, after a few moments, added; "because of the Jewish community that lived here, in the Chalkwell Hall Estate. You know, they planned out two estates in Chalkwell: the Hall Estate and the Chalkwell Park Estate. Luckily they changed their minds about the Chalkwell Park Estate and kept it green."

"That was lucky," I said. "Chalkwell Park's a great place to wind down on sunny Sunday afternoons."

"I wouldn't know about that," said Uncle Fred, with a grin. "I go on Wednesday mornings."

We shared a laugh.

"At one time there was talk of renaming Westcliff," he went on. "The name had slowly evolved from being, literally, the west cliff of Southend, and I think someone wanted to give it a proper name. Do you know what they came up with?"

I shook my head and waited.

"Kensington-on-Sea," he said, with a smile. "Eventually they abandoned the idea. The estate names aren't known these days, but the town was divided into several different estates. The area between Milton Road and Park Street was the Park Estate, because it was built on

Southend Park, which had a lake and several playing fields. There was Beach Estate, which was the area from Palmerston Road to Whitefriars Crescent. Next to this was Clifton Estate - Clifton Drive, Manor Road and Seaforth Road. Then there was the Hamlet Estate, east of Hamlet Court Road, which was also known as 'The Hamlet'; the West Cliff Park Estate, with Westborough Road running through it; and the Somerset Gardens Estate, which was built up between the wars, off Bridgwater Drive. There was another, but I've forgotten it."

"So which of them were you born in?" I asked.

"Just a minute," said Uncle Fred, thoughtfully. "I'm trying to remember that other estate. Was it Clifton?"

"You've already mentioned Clifton."

"Of course. I know. It was North Clifton. This was around Valkyrie Road. And, while I'm on Valkyrie Road, I'll tell you why it was so named. That and Britannia Road, Satanita Road, Genesta Road, Meteor Road and Ailsa Road were named after the giant yachts, which sailed around the coast of Britain in 1893 and visited Southend - amongst other places - on their travels. My father told me it was a spectacular sight."

"Tell me, Uncle Fred, what was Westcliff like when you were born?"

"Well," he said, then shrugged his shoulders and added, simply; "different."

"You were born in Westcliff though, were you?"

"I was born in Inverness Avenue. April it was. There was thick snow on the ground, and you could see St Mary's Church in Prittlewell from our back windows."

"What year was that?"

"I'd better go and pour the tea out."

So Uncle Fred went back into the kitchenette, and when he returned he changed the subject. Curiosity drove me to the library a few days later, where I searched through weather records and found April snow in the years 1891, 1908, 1913 and 1919. He surely couldn't have been born in the last century, and there would have been houses in 1919 to obstruct the view of St Mary's. So Uncle Fred was born in 1908 or 1913.

When he plonked the cup of tea down on the coffee table in front of me, half of it spilled into the saucer and he didn't notice. So I had to scrape constantly the bottom of the cup on the edge of the saucer, and put my hand beneath the cup as I drank to stop the drips falling onto my lap. Uncle Fred has since told all the family about my peculiar way of drinking a cup of tea.

"In those days," he continued, "a builder would build a house pretty much where he wanted, and services were put on afterwards. The bricks were pulled in a cart with two horses, but the ruts in the road got so deep that a spare horse had to be harnessed up to help.

People like Mr Dowsett, Mr Ingram, Mr Ramuz and Mr Townsend wanted to develop the town so they erected a great marquee opposite the Palace Theatre where auctions were held to sell off chunks of land. I say `opposite the Palace Theatre' but it wasn't actually there at the time. All this was about a hundred years ago. There was a farmhouse there, Barlands, it was called. Have a look at the map. You'll see it there."

I put my cup into the saucer pond and got up. As I stepped across the room, he added; "And that picture two to the left of the map is the actual place. Lovely, isn't it?"

It was indeed. I found it difficult to believe

Barlands

that this delightful old house could have once stood just behind where now stand a bank, a car showroom, and a supermarket, between Ramuz Drive and Brightwell Avenue. I made a suitable comment to express my thoughts.

"I'll tell you what I know about it," said Uncle Fred. "It was called Barlands Farm or sometimes Green Shutters Farm. The house had a parlour, living room, kitchen, dairy, cellar and four bedrooms. Then there were the barns, granaries, pens and stables. The farm was about one hundred and forty acres of arable meadow and pasture land, and went as far as Nelson Road. The Prittle Brook ran through some of the fields. Can you imagine the cows slurping away at the water in the brook? Because that's how it would have been."

"It's difficult," I said. The brook now runs behind garden fences, and is lined with concrete.

"Anyway; of its history. In 1577 the tenant was one Henry Butler, who rented it from Sir Robert Rich for the princely sum of sixteen pounds, six shillings and eight pence a year. That's sixteen pounds and thirty-three pence to you, lad." He smiled. "In 1858 Daniel Scratton leased it to Mr A. Bentall for £296 a year, but in 1871 it was sold to Sir A. Neave who continued to lease it to Mr Bentall at the lesser sum of £250. So I'd imagine that Mr Bentall was rather pleased about that particular sale. The earliest date I know of it is in 1469 when it was mentioned in the will of John Quyk, although it ws probably named after Sir William Barlond, who held land in Prittlewell in the seventh year of Richard II, which I reckon comes out at 1384. The house was demolished around the turn of the century."

"And that's it?" I asked.

"Yes; that's all I know about Barlands."

"I'm amazed that you know all this stuff," I said. "How do you manage to remember all those dates and amounts of money? Can't be word association."

"Just do," replied Uncle Fred. "Don't ask me what I did last week, or when my next appointment is at the dentist, or when Betty's due again to give this place the once over. Ask me those questions and I won't give you an answer. But ask me about the legend of King Canute and..."

He was interrupted by a knock at the door. Five rapid knocks, then the door was opened from the outside and a beaming woman burst noisily into the room.

"'Ello, Fred," she said. "I've come to give your place the once over. 'Ello? Who's this?"

"Hello, Betty," said Uncle Fred. They were grinning at each other as if they'd been friends for many years; as if they knew that the other would make them laugh hysterically at any moment.

"This is my great-nephew. At this particular moment in time I seem to have forgotten his name. Sorry, lad."

He laughed, she laughed, and I smiled and introduced myself.

"Do us one o' your cuppas, will you, Fred?" she ordered in a cheerful way.

"Course I will, Bet," said Uncle Fred, and went back to the kitchenette. Betty went to a corner cupboard, opened it and took out a duster, a furniture polish aerosol, and a vacuum cleaner.

"So 'ow you keeping, Fred?" she inquired.

"Fine thanks, Betty. Fine. And you?"

"Me?" she said. "Me? you know me, Fred. I'm always fine. Always 'appy. Always Betty."

"So you won't be wanting a nip of brandy in your tea," said Fred.

Cliffs Bandstand

Betty laughed loudly. Very, very loudly, then said; "No, but I'll 'ave the brandy to chase the tea down."

As Uncle Fred laughed, Betty turned to me. "So," she said. "What's 'e been telling yer?"

"He's telling me the history of Westcliff," I said. "I didn't realise there was so much of it."

"Yeh, yeh," she said, offhandedly. "'E's told me that once or twice. Has 'e said the serfs didn't ride waves?"

"Yes."

"And has 'e told you about the fellah with the 'ard boiled egg?"

"Yes."

"And has 'e told you about the Fol de Rols?"

"The foldy what?"

"Rols."

"No, he hasn't. Uncle Fred," I called. "You haven't told me about the Fol de Rols."

"It'll 'ave to wait, I'm afraid," said Betty. "I'm doing the 'oovering now."

And with that she plugged it in, switched it on and put a temporary halt to Uncle Fred's history of Westcliff-on-Sea.

Chalkwell Park entrance, 1931

V

When Betty had finished the vacuum cleaning, she stood in the centre of the room with the duster, the polish and a saucer in her left hand, and the tea cup in her right. From time to time she slurped her tea.

"My dad used to take me down to Fol de Rols when I was little," said Uncle Fred. "Then we'd go on down to the sea-front where we played hoop-la."

"So what was Fol de Rols?" I asked.

"It was an entertainment hall on the cliffs," he explained. "Also known as the Floral Hall. It burnt down just before the war - about 1937, I believe. Who played there? I only remember two or three acts now. Gertie Gitana was one, Uncle Alf another, and er..."

"Doris somebody," said Betty.

"Yes, Doris..." confirmed Uncle Fred.

"What sort of entertainment was it?" I asked.

"Well you know. A bit of everything. Like `Sunday Night at the London Palladium'. Comedians, singers, little sketches, dance routines. At that time I went to a private school at Miss Chappell's in Albion Road, clutching a shilling to pay her on Monday mornings. We had to sing our tables every morning right up to the twelve. And we wrote with chalk on slates."

"I bet that was noisy," commented Betty, then drank the last of her tea, put the cup to the saucer with a loud clatter and put the two into the kitchen sink with a louder clatter. She then proceeded to polish the surfaces.

"The reason I mentioned that," said Uncle Fred, "was that on sunny afternoons my friend Arthur and I would run straight from school down to the cliffs and play there until the sun

Shorefield House

went down. Sometimes we'd play football or cricket on the fields at the bottom of Chalkwell Avenue, or if we were lucky we'd see Happy Harry."

"Who was Happy Harry?"

"He was an evangelist who'd walk along the seafront and stop from time to time to do some preaching with his hat on the floor for the collection of money. Some people would wrap farthings in silver paper to make them look like sixpences. But the funniest thing is when he prayed - eyes closed, looking sincere and pious - and one of us children would yell out; `Harry! They're pinching your money!' and he'd snap out of his praying and chase us down the road. Happy Harry's real name was Reverend George Wood and there is a small plaque on the sea wall opposite Southend's arcades dedicated to him. He died in 1974 at the age of 86."

"Fred," said Betty, when she'd recovered from a short burst of coughing, "Tell 'im 'ow long it took 'em to build the Cliffs Pavilion."

She seemed to finish this sentence with a hiss, but it turned out to be the sound of her spraying the aerosol on the surface of the mahogany-effect display cabinet, on which there were no ornaments, only an old, framed photograph of Aunt Sissy. "Go on, Fred, tell 'im."

"Twenty seven years," said Uncle Fred.

"What!" I exclaimed. "Twenty seven years! Why did it take so long?"

"Well." Uncle Fred leaned back in his chair. "Let's see. There was a place called Shorefield House, in which lived Frederick Ramuz, the Mayor at one time, who I mentioned earlier, with his wife and ten children. There was a little orchard where San Remo Parade is now. Also Southend's first printing press was established there in the nineteenth century by

SOUTHENDIANA;

OR,

BAGATELLE,

PRODUCED IN THE SEASON OF

1823,

AT SOUTHEND.

———◦———

Molte gran cose in picciol fascio stringo. PETR.

PRITTLEWELL:

The title page of *Southendiana* by Frederick Nolan, 1823

Dr Frederic Nolan. The land to the east of the house was used as a brick and tile field in the 1790s when they were building the new Southend. It was let by Daniel Scratton to the builders for four years on condition that they 'levelled and made good for husbandry' the land when they'd finished."

"Have you got a dictionary, Uncle Fred?" I asked with a smile.

"Husbandry means farming," he said, anticipating my question.

"Thank you."

"So. The council bought the site in 1935 and had plans drawn up. In '37 they started work at an estimated cost of £45,000. It was going to be a hexagonal building. Then came the war and it all stopped. It wasn't until 1954 that they brought it up again, agreed on a price of £125,000, but revised it, and agreed to a new design in 1956 at a cost of £210,000. Next a financial crisis came along and it was all postponed for a time. Talks resumed the following year when there was a tender for £211,000, but the council rejected this, so more debates and a complete review. Finally they designed the building in 1959, making use of the original foundations, started work and, at long last, completed it in 1964. It was opened by the actor Bernard Miles in July and the first show was *Coppelia* by the Ballet Rambert."

"The Ballet Rambert," said Betty, holding the duster by one corner and twirling it round while humming tunelessly. Uncle Fred and I laughed at this.

"So," said Uncle Fred, thoughtfully. "Ah, yes. Talking of debates, disputes and disagreements in general, have I told you about the dispute between the villagers of Milton Hamlet and Prittlewell?"

"No you haven't," I said.

"There's not much to tell," Betty piped in. "Mind if I tell it, Fred?"

"No; go ahead, Bet."

"Right then. It was about a thousand years ago..."

"It was in 1678, Bet," corrected Uncle Fred.

"1678, a thousand years ago, what's the difference?"

"Carry on, Bet" said Uncle Fred, smiling.

"Right, I will. It was 1678, I do believe, when this old bridge was knackered out, where Victoria Avenue goes over the brook (though Victoria Avenue was called North Street in them days). Don't even notice the bridge these days, but then it was a little footbridge. Wagons and 'orses 'ad to take their chances through the brook. So, anyway, it was knackered and it 'ad to be fixed, and o' course someone 'ad to pay for the fixing of it. Now the Prittlewell lot reckoned the Milton lot should chip in, but the Milton lot reckoned it 'ad nothing to do with them and it was down to the Prittlewell lot. So the Prittlewellians 'ad themselves a meeting where this bloke called Thankless spoke up and..."

"Unthank, Bet," said Uncle Fred. "His name was Josias Unthank."

"Right. So this bloke called Josias Unthank spoke up and said they should get an order to make the Milton lot chip in. And that's it."

"But did they get the order?" I asked. "Did the Milton lot chip in?"

Betty shrugged.

"We don't know the outcome," said Uncle Fred. "It wasn't recorded."

"Shame," I said. "A story without an ending."

"Did I tell it all right, Fred?" asked Betty.

"Perfectly," said Uncle Fred. "I couldn't have told it better myself."

"And I didn't miss anything out?"

"Not a thing."

"Right then, I'm done. I've finished the 'oovering and the polishing, I've told a bit of your story and I've 'ad a cup a'tea. So I'll be off."

"Righto, Bet," said Uncle Fred. "Thanks. I'll see you next time."

"Monday," said Betty. "Usual time. Nice meeting you, young man. 'Ope you enjoy the rest of the story."

"Thanks," I said."Nice meeting you, too."

"See ya then," she said. "See ya Monday, Fred. 'Bye!" And off she went, leaving me with the impression that she and Uncle Fred would have chatted and laughed more if I hadn't been there.

"What does she mean, `usual time'?" he said. "I'm sure she doesn't have a usual time."

"Well," I said, "if it's any help, I think she came at about two o'clock today."

"Thanks, lad. I'll try to keep it in mind." But I could see from his expression that he was already half way towards forgetting it.

"So," I said. "Is there any more to this history of Westcliff-on-Sea?"

"A little. Go and look at the map again and tell me what I haven't mentioned."

Chalkwell Avenue, 193:

48

VI

"What about this one up here?" I said. "Colemans Farm."

"Ah, yes, Colemans Farm," said Uncle Fred. "Well, you know where that was, don't you?"

"No."

"It was on what is now the junction of Colemans Avenue and Fairview Drive. It had a drawing room, a dining room, kitchen, dairy, pantry and four bedrooms," said Uncle Fred. "Plus stables. There isn't much history attached to it, I'm afraid. John Coleman owned the farm in 1304, and it was mentioned in 1577 as being in the tenure of Nicholas Glascock. The house was demolished in 1970. If you look to the north-west of it on the map you'll see 'Old Oak'. This was a huge tree on the farm which marked the boundary between Prittlewell and Eastwood. In the nineteenth century this tree was badly damaged but survived a fire, caused by a the carelessness of a crow boy. How he managed to set fire to it, I don't know."

"Where exactly was it?" I asked.

"On the junction of what is now Northville Drive and Prince Avenue. You know, I used to stroll through Coleman's cornfields on my way to church on Sunday mornings. Or, in autumn I'd go down Hobleythick Lane picking blackberries as I went. Often went blackberrying in Hobleythick Lane."

This brought images to mind of country lanes and open fields on a sunny day. The farmhouse in the middle-distance, the sound of bird-song, of horses' hooves and squeaky cartwheels, where now you're surrounded by houses, car engines and exhaust fumes.

"Hobleythick Lane, in those days," continued Uncle Fred, "ran along what is now Chase Gardens at its southern end. The part of Hobleythick parallel to this was called Osnaburg Gardens. And that little stretch of

Prittlewell Chase was once part of Hillborough Road. Talking of old road names, do you know that little street, near the Cricketers' pub, called Summercourt Road?"

I did.

"Well that used to go right through, into Salisbury Road, and had streets called Newlands Road, Eastwick Road and Campbell Road going east to North Road. They all went when they built those flats."

"You mean Brecon, Grampian and Blackdown?"

"Yes. And as I mentioned the Cricketers', it was named so because there used to be a cricket pitch just across Milton Road from it. It was opened as an inn in 1866 having previously been two cottages. The town's fire engine was kept in one of the pub's outhouses, because the publican was a part-time fireman. They used the engine as a hearse when he died, a year or two before the first world war."

"I still find it amazing, Uncle Fred, that you can remember all this. You've got a fantastic memory."

"Not really, lad," said Uncle Fred. "Don't ask me what I did last week, or when my next appointment is with the dentist, or when Betty's next due to give this place the once over. I won't know the answers. Have I already said that?"

"You have, yes."

"But ask me about the legend of King Canute and I'll tell you."

There was a brief silence before I asked: "So, what is the legend of King Canute?"

"Thought you'd never ask, lad. In the early part of the eleventh century, Canute was in Essex. Legend has it that, after the battle of Ashingdon, he sat on the Milton shore and ordered the waves to stop advancing, in order to prove that he couldn't do it and put a stop to the endless flattery from his courtiers."

Chalkwell Hall, c.1900

"And that's the legend of King Canute?"

"It is," said Uncle Fred. "And of course the Danes were here also, even if they were only passing through. Coincidentally, they were camped at a place called Milton in Kent, over the river from Tilbury. In 893, after the battles of Farnham and Benfleet, they fled across Hadleigh, Leigh, Middleton, and Southchurch before setting up a camp in Shoeburyness."

"Middleton being the old name for Milton," I said, checking the details.

"That's right."

"So," I said. "Have any more roads disappeared or changed their names?"

"Ah! Yes. I've digressed. Yes. Hamlet Court Road. Like so many English roads, Hamlet Court Road went square round two sides of a field before going down to the sharp bend over the railway. Eventually they straightened it and named the original route Ditton Court Road. Then the northern half of Hamlet Court Road was called Sallendines Lane. Shorefield Road was Occupation Road, and Holland Road was Piccadilly Road at the bottom of which was Piccadilly Steps leading down to the sea-front."

"They've certainly changed it all around," I commented. "Can you tell me something that I've occasionally wondered about?"

"What's that, lad?"

"Why are there streets in Westcliff with `Eastwood' in the name which are nowhere near the place?"

"That's simple," replied Uncle Fred. "There was a lane leading from Chalkwell Hall to Eastwood, called Eastwood Lane. Once again, it took a staggered route around the fields. Down Southbourne Grove as far as Eastwood Lane South, into Eastwood Boulevard, along Kenilworth Gardens, round the little access road into Westcliff High School, then up Mountdale Gardens and Treecot Drive. And one of my pictures is of the lane, looking down

52

The Front

Southbourne Grove from the gates of Chalkwell Hall in about 1900."

It was unrecognisable. Nothing but trees. I noticed a picture of the one building that's still standing, although its surroundings have clearly changed.

"And what can you tell me about Chalkwell Hall?" I asked, tapping the print with my finger. Unfortunately, my tapping made it fall, but surprisingly, it didn't break when it hit the carpet.

"You great idiot," said Uncle Fred, but not angrily.

"Sorry, Uncle Fred," I said. "I'll put it back."

But the string had come away from the hook. I began to tie it back on.

"Before you destroy it completely, I'd better tell you about the place," said Uncle Fred. "The name Chalkwell comes - as the name implies - from a well lined with chalk which was about five hundred feet west of the hall. It's on the map, if you want to look."

"Later," I said. "This is an awkward little job."

"Fine. There was once a mound on the estate, east of the house, in a corner of a field called Fishponds. It was opened in about 1860 and its treasures consisted of a few bones, a piece of chain and some coins, all thought to be of Celtic origin.

"There have been at least two Chalkwell Halls. The previous building was south-west of the present one in a field called Moat Field, on the Leigh Road, but this was demolished in 1832. It is thought that it once had a deep, wide moat around it, and I've always thought that this is how the Ridgeway came by its name.

"The earliest mention of the place is 1478 when it was occupied by a Robert Swete. The present hall was built in 1830 by Mr George Mason."

Uncle Fred stopped momentarily and chuckled to himself.

"There's a little story attached to George Mason that I always find rather amusing," he said. "Apparently his great-grandfather, on his mother's side, was a Frenchman living in England. He clearly couldn't get the hang of our English customs, because he once said: 'If I say to this man, "I give you my horse," he says, "thank you." And if to another, "I give you this piece of furniture," he says, "thank you". But if I say, "I give you my daughter," he says, "and what will you give with her?"'

Uncle Fred chuckled more before adding, "And that's the brief history of Chalkwell Hall. Except of course that the council bought it with twenty-six-and-a-half acres of land for £20,000 in the summer of 1901."

He reached over to the occasional table beside his chair and picked up his pipe.

Station Road

Prittlewell Pest House

VII

When at last I'd finished tying the string onto the hook, Uncle Fred was filling his pipe with tobacco.

"What else is there, Uncle Fred?"

"Eh? What do you mean?" he asked, concentrating fully on his pipe.

"The history of Westcliff."

"Ah, yes. Well, there's Clatterfields. Another farm, sold off just before the Great War as a `building estate ripe for immediate development'. At the time there was a cottage and gardens facing Eastwood Lane, or Boulevard, just about where the White Hall now stands. Of course it's a street now - Clatterfield Gardens."

He continued the filling of his pipe. "Very near to this was Prittlewell Pest House, which stood roughly at the end of what's now Cavendish Gardens. Pest houses were hospitals for people with infectious diseases, like the dreaded smallpox, built in the eighteenth century away from the towns or villages they served. Some time in the first half of the nineteenth century this one had stopped being used as such and had been converted into two homes. It was a timber-framed building which became run down and was demolished in 1914.

"But there was another isolation hospital in Prittlewell which was inadequate for the town, so in 1893 the council built a new sanatorium at the end of Balmoral Road for patients with diseases like scarlet fever, typhoid, tuberculosis and diphtheria. That's a nasty little group of diseases, if you ask me. No-one - patients or staff - was allowed to leave the hospital until they'd been thoroughly disinfected, and in those days that probably meant a good scrub down with carbolic acid, hot water and a wire brush."

He paused for a few moments while we both laughed. "My father once told me of the great pandemonium it caused in the streets when they took someone to the hospital. Until 1898 the patients were taken in a hand-litter followed by a crowd of children and curious adults. An old chap in his seventies pulled it along from the front, a nurse walked on one side, a gentleman on the other, and two more men pushed from the back. One of these had a wooden leg, would you believe? Then, every now and again, the whole lot of them would stop so that the nurse could check that the patient was all right!"

Uncle Fred chuckled again at this image. "Later, of course, these diseases became less common and the hospital was adapted for the care of elderly patients. In the 1950s it was renamed Westcliff Hospital. There was another hospital on the corner of Kings Road and Seymour Road. From 1907 to 1940 it was a residential home called St Ursula's, but in 1951 it re-opened as the Victoria Hospital for surgical patients and was used until 1974. I believe it was demolished in the early 1980s."

"Yeh, I vaguely remember that being there," I said. "Didn't know it was a hospital though."

"Throw me those matches, will you, lad?" said Uncle Fred. I did as he asked, and he went through the process of lighting the pipe but managed to say out of the corner of his mouth, "I shouldn't be smoking while talking about hospitals, should I."

The aroma instantly filled the room, as the smoke drifted upwards and settled above his head. "And then, of course, the biggest hospital in Westcliff is the Southend General. Do you want me to tell you about that?"

I did.

"The original Southend Hospital was the Victoria in Warrior Square which, by 1923, had grown too small for Southend. After some lengthy discussion Lord Iveagh, the MP at the time, went and bought the site along Prittlewell

Chase, which was part of Coleman's Farm. This was something he did without ceremony, at his own expense, and other wealthy people in the town followed his example by making donations towards the cost of the hospital."

"This is a Member of Parliament we're talking about, is it?" I inquired. "Not a Military Policeman."

"Yes, it is."

"Sounds like a nice fellow."

"Yes, he does, and there's more to come. It took four years for the money to be raised, and the foundation stone was laid in November, 1929, by the Duchess of York, now the Queen Mother. Incidentally, the royal car got there via Ramuz Drive and Springfield Drive. The hospital was finally opened in July 1932, by Lord and Lady Iveagh. It was announced at the opening ceremony that £51,000 was still needed and Lord Iveagh instantly pledged it.

"The foundation stone for Southend Victoria Hospital, dated from 13th August 1887, was moved from the old to the new hospital and is now just outside the entrance. Again, as the years went by, the hospital grew too small for the town, so they built the new block which was opened by Princess Anne in 1971, though it was already in use by this time."

"That's the tower block on the right as you look at it," I inquired.

"Yes, that's it."

"And what about the even newer block?"

"What even newer block?" asked Uncle Fred.

"The one they just recently opened on the left as you look at it," I said.

"Did they?"

"Yes; didn't you know, Uncle Fred?"

"No, I didn't. What's it like?"

"It's good. Nicer than the tower block. They've made it in keeping with the old part. In fact, you can hardly see the joins."

"Well, lad, you'll have to show it to me some

The Crowstone

time. I'd like to see it."

"I will, Uncle Fred."

A few moments of silence passed while Uncle Fred puffed on his pipe, apparently coming to terms with his not knowing of this recent development.

"Do you know about the Crowstone?" he asked. It was a complete change of subject and one which, I'd imagine, he made to get back onto familiar ground.

"Not really, Uncle Fred," I replied. "It's something to do with the end of the Thames, is it?"

"In a way, it is," said Uncle Fred. "The first Crowstone was erected in 1285 to mark the limit of the City of London's jurisdiction over the Thames. It was visited every seven years by the Lord Mayor of London and his name carved into it. There was a similar stone on the Kent side of the river."

"You mean like St Michael's Mount," I observed. "One off the coast of Cornwall, and another on the French side of the Channel."

"Yes, I suppose so," said Uncle Fred, looking a little amused by my observation. "Only much smaller."

He paused for a puff. "The original Crowstone," he continued, "was replaced by a new one in 1755, and this replaced in 1837 by a taller stone made of granite, which is the one still there. After the Second World War the 1755 stone was taken to Priory Park, where it still stands, next to the priory. If you go there you can see some well-worn figures carved into it but they can't be read. But if you go to the drawer over there, you'll find a piece of paper with some names and dates."

I got up and stepped to the drawer, while Uncle Fred continued; "This is what was legible on two sides of the Crowstone in 1824, when an interesting little book called *A Guide To Southend* was written."

Westcliff Station, 1902

I had opened the drawer and found the paper, on which was scribbled:

Brass Crosby, Esq. 1771
Richard Clark, Esq. 1785
William Gill, Esq. 1789
William Curtis, Esq. 1796
Sir John Eamer, Knt. 1802
Charles Flower, Esq. 1809
Matthew Wood, Esq. 1816
William Heygate, Esq. 1823

"Didn't you say it was every seven years?" I asked.

"Yes, I did," said Uncle Fred. "I think they must have used British Rail. Richard Clark arrived so late and William Gill so early that I think they almost met at the station."

We shared another laugh.

"But of course that can't be," said Uncle Fred. "Chalkwell didn't have a railway station until 1933, and Westcliff station opened in 1894. And the railway itself didn't come this way until 1854.

"Just one more thing about the Crowstone. It's a good indication to the amount of land lost to the sea over the years, because the first Crowstone was actually on the shoreline, but it's now some distance offshore. And, by the way, the last mayor to visit the stone was David Salomons, Esquire, in 1856."

"Can I ask why it's called the Crowstone?"

"Certainly. Quite simply, it was originally erected on a field called Crowes Field. Would you like another cup of tea, lad?"

"Another?"

"Yes, another."

I might die of tea poisoning, but Uncle Fred's tea is just too good to refuse.

VIII

The cups of tea were this time accompanied on a tray by two very large fresh-cream meringues. Uncle Fred smiled, a faintly wicked smile, and raised his eyebrows. "They must be eaten today, or they'll go off," he said.

"That's all right with me," I said. "Fresh-cream meringues are my favourite, as it happens."

"Mine too," said Uncle Fred, placing the tray on the coffee table. Little did I know that I would end up not eating mine in the rush.

"That baker round the corner is very good, you know," he went on. "It reminds me of the baker of my youth. He'd come down the street, crying out `Baker! Baker!'. Of course you probably wouldn't know this, but bread was sold by the pound and if a loaf wasn't quite enough he'd cut a piece from another loaf, and that piece was called the make-weight."

He sat down. "And then there was the milkman. 'Milko! Milko!' he'd yell, pushing his three-wheeled handcart on which he had a big brass milk-churn. Hanging around the sides were the milk cans, rattling away, that he used when he measured out the milk. We'd all run out there with our jugs and he'd fill them up for us."

"Did he have separate milk-churns for skimmed and semi-skimmed?" I asked, facetiously.

"Course not, you great idiot. In those days milk was just milk. There were great big slabs of butter and cheese in Stockwell's the grocer, on the corner of Valkyrie Road and London Road. When I asked for it he'd cut it with the wire and wrap it in greaseproof paper. Mr Stockwell had a cat that would wander around the shop and sleep on top of the biscuit tins.

The Shepherd's Cot

One day I took our dog in and she spotted the cat. Well, I must say, things got a bit chaotic from then on. The dog started barking, the cat started hissing, Mr Stockwell started panicking and the next thing I knew there were biscuit tins clattering all over the place. Took me ages to put them back again."

Uncle Fred paused for a chuckle and reached over for his meringue. He looked at it for a few moments, dipped his tongue in the cream, and appeared to enjoy this immensely. "Most of the shops were down in Hamlet Court Road, as they are still," he continued. "There was Radio Rentals - still there I believe."

I nodded and glanced at my cake.

"Sissy used to get her hair done at Craddock's, we'd buy our shoes at Jennings', and there was Wixley's the jeweller, a little sweet shop called Bryn's, and several drapers - Bartlett's, Knight's..."

It seemed as though he was going to list a few more, but a new thought had struck him. "Knight's was on the corner where Pollard's was until recently," he said. "But once upon a time there stood in that place a cottage called `The Shepherd's Cottage', also known as `Shepherd's Cot'. It was built by Robert Scratton for his shepherd, John Dowsett, in about 1870, but was demolished after Dowsett's wife died in 1912, Dowsett himself having died some years earlier.

"There was a thatched cottage on the corner of Milton Road, across from the Cricketers' Inn. Now we're getting down into the heart of the old hamlet - mainly the land between Milton Road and Hamlet Court Road. There were several farms and houses down there. I was on Wickford Road the other day and noticed that there's a new Doric Lodge on the site of the old Doric Lodge, which stood for many years there.

Hamlet Court

Then there was Hamlet Cottage, Hamlet Lodge and Hamlet House; Milton House, Grove House and Shorefield House. Hamlet House was also known as Hamlet Court, and that's how it looked."

He pointed casually up at the wall, but looked only at his meringue. As I studied his print of Hamlet Court - another lovely old ivy-clad building with a family posing formally outside - I heard him shovel another tongueful of cream into his mouth.

"It was built about 1800 and demolished in 1929. Sir Edwin Arnold and Robert Williams Buchanan lived in that house," he said, stickily. "At different times, of course."

"Who were they?"

"Arnold was an author, famous for *The Light of Asia*, a poem in blank verse published in 1879. He wrote a lot of other books, including some about the British administration in India, where he'd previously lived for about five years. He was so highly regarded that he was considered as a succcessor to the Poet Laureateship after Alfred, Lord Tennyson died in 1892. He actually moved into Hamlet Court in 1878.

"In 1885 Robert Buchanan, a poet, novelist, satirist and playwright, took up residence there. He wrote of the area, `there is no lovelier spot when the Spring becomes a certainty'. Later he moved to Byculla House, on the cliffs. His best known poem was called *The City of Dreams*.

"While we're on the subject of writers, the novelist Mrs Coulson Kernahan lived just round the corner in Preston Road, in a house anmed `Thrums'. She was an admirer of J M Barrie, who had given the name Thrums to his birthplace, Kirriemuir, which was the setting for some of his early work. I believe the house is still called Thrums."

Uncle Fred paused for breath, before getting back to Hamlet Court Road.

"Hamlet Lodge was on the junction of what is now Anerley Road. It was previously a farm called Snell's which was advertised for sale in 1827 as being 'within one-and-a-half miles of that increasing fashionable bathing place, Southend'.

"Then there was Greenings, a small farm which was all but lost to the sea, and Thompson's Farm - which later became Vincent's Farm - near the windmill. Hence the name of St Vincent's Road. Again, one field on this farm called Washers was reduced from five acres to three acres because of the encroachment of the sea."

He paused for a moment, appearing to think deeply. "And that's all," he said. "The history of Westcliff-on-Sea and Milton Hamlet."

"Thanks, Uncle Fred. That was really interesting," I said, and went back for one last look at the map. "But what's this?" I said. "Bobbetshole?"

"Ah yes, of course," said Uncle Fred. "Bobbets Hole. As you can see, it was in the area of St Helen's Road. It was previously called Little Groomes, and belonged to a family called Morrison. I mention this only because, in the eighteenth century, a daughter in that house, Sarah, married the ludicrously named Reverend Morice Morice."

As I laughed, Uncle Fred took a large bite from his meringue. White crumbs cascaded down into his lap and on to his chair. I think I now realised why I had delayed biting into mine.

"In about 1869 St Helen's Church was built on the farm and the old farmhouse was demolished about 1880. And that leads me on

The Playground.
St Bernard's Convent School Westcliff-on-Sea.

St Bernard's Convent School playgrounds

to the schools in the area."

"Why's that?"

"Well, in a roundabout way, St Helen's Church is where St Bernard's High School was started. Do you want me to tell you about it?"

Of course I did, and said so as Uncle Fred put his half-eaten cake on to the plate.

"St Bernard's was started as St Mary's Convent, in the house behind St Helen's, by the Sisters of Notre Dame of Munich, who'd come down from London to live in the fresh air. This was in 1869. In 1875 they bought the Hotel Mitre, on the corner of Canewdon Road and Milton Road, but in 1910 they left and were replaced by the Bernardine Sisters from Slough. The following year they changed the name to St Bernard's.

"In the meantime, in 1899, a new school was opened in the house behind St Helen's, called St Helen's School, but in 1973 they moved to the new building in North Road. Which school did you go to, lad?"

"Chalkwell."

"Do you know when it was built?"

"If I did, I've forgotten."

"1909. Before that there was Hamlet Court School, built in 1896, extended a few years later, and demolished a few years ago. And guess what's there now."

"Flats?"

"A car park, on the old playground. You can still see cricket stumps and targets painted on the walls. Sad that."

He picked up the meringue, held it in front of his face and put it down again. Although he said nothing, it seemed from his expression that it had almost, but not quite, jogged something in his recent memory.

"Now, the largest private school in the area was the Lindisfarne College in Valkyrie Road,"

Lindisfarne College, 1905

he said, shrugging off whatever it was that was almost bothering him. "It was built in 1898 and had a five-acre sports field in Crowstone Road, which was recently built on. They had day boys and boarders. The boarders had to have a swim and a brisk walk every day before breakfast, which was served at 7.30.

"In 1921 they erected a Memorial for the Old Boys who died in the Great War; it was a copy of the Crowstone, because they had seen it every day on their morning walk. I remember in 1936 there was a big fire at the school. The roof fell in but no-one was hurt. Mind you, one lad got a bit of a shock when he was squirted in the face by another boy wielding a fire extinguisher! The building's still there but it's now a leisure centre."

"Do you know when the other schools came about?" I asked.

"Certainly do," replied Uncle Fred, but before he could reveal this information, the telephone rang. It was on the occasional table, beside the ashtray and behind the meringue; Uncle Fred picked it up. "Yes?" he said, and listened for a few moments. I could hear that it was a woman.

"Oh blimey," he said. "Terribly sorry. I'll leave right away. Be there in fifteen minutes. Thank you. Bye-bye." He put the phone down and looked up at me. "I was supposed to be at the dentist's twenty-five minutes ago. I'd better hurry."

"Don't worry, Uncle Fred. I'll give you a lift down there."

"That's kind of you, lad. I'll brush my teeth. Blasted bits of meringue everywhere."

He left the room and, a few minutes later, his echoing voice continued from the bathroom, with the sound of running water in the background. "Westborough School," he called, "was opened in 1912. Westcliff High moved to Westcliff from Victoria Avenue in 1926 and Fairfax opened three years later. Just a minute."

As I put the meringues back into his fridge, I heard the unmistakable sound of teeth being hastily brushed, of a mouth being violently rinsed, and of water being spat into a wash-hand basin.

"Earl's Hall School was opened in 1938, but closed for the following year because of the war." He was obviously now calling while smothering his mouth with a towel. "And in the 1960s Baron's Court and Milton Hall Schools were opened."

There was a moment's silence, then Uncle Fred was standing in the doorway, putting on his coat. "And that," he said, "concludes my history of Westcliff-on-Sea."

"It was great, Uncle Fred," I said. "I still don't know how you remember all that stuff."

"Come on, lad," he said. "Don't worry about the lift. I'll take the Jag."

From the *Southend Standard*, 4 June 1875

74

INDEX

Page numbers printed in italics relate to illustrations

Ailsa Road 35
Albion Road 42
Anerley Road 69
Arnold, Edwin 68
Arnold, Thomas 12
Asplin, Jonas 23
Avenue Road 12
Balmoral Road 57
Bandstand *26,28,40*
Barlands Farm 36,*37*
Barlond, William 38
Baron's Court School 74
Bartlett's 66
Beedell Avenue 2,19
Bentall, A 38
Bobbetshole 69
Bridge House *17,18*
Bridgwater Drive 35
Brightwell Avenue 38
Britannia Road 35
Bryn's 66
Buchanan, Robert W 68
Butler, Henry 38
Byam family 16

Campbell Road 50
Canewdon Road 71
Cannon Cinema 6
Canute, King 50
Cavendish Gardens 57
Chalkwell Avenue 44,*48*
Chalkwell Hall *51,52*
Chalkwell Hall Estate 34
Chalkwell Park 34
Chalkwell School 71
Chalkwell Station 63
Chappell, Miss 42
Chase Gardens 49
Clark, Richard 63
Classic Cinema 6
Clatterfield Gardens 57
Clatterfields 57
Cliffs Pavilion 44
Clifton Drive 35
Clifton Estate 35
Coleman, John 48
Coleman's Farm 48,58
Colemans Avenue 48
Craddock's 66
Cricketers' 50,66
Crosby, Brass 63
Crowes Field 63
Crowstone *60,61*

Crowstone Road 73
Curtis, William 63
D'Aranda family 23
Ditton Court Road 52
Dolphinarium 25
Doric Lodge 66
Dowsett, John 66
Dowsett, Mr 36
Eamer, John 63
Earl's Hall School 74
Eastwick Road 50
Eastwood Boulevard 52
Eastwood Lane 52,57
Essoldo Cinema 6
Fairfax Drive 18
Fairview Drive 49
Fire Station 50
Fishponds 54
Floral Hall 42
Flower, Charles 63
Fol de Rols 41,42
Frith, John 14
Gainsborough Drive 18
Genesta Road 35
Gill, William 63
Gitana, Gertie 42
Glascock, Nicholas 49
Green Shutters Farm 38

Greening's Farm 69
Grove House 68
Hamlet Windmill 12,*13*
Hamlet Cottage 68
Hamlet Court *67,68*
Hamlet Court Road 4,*5*,6,35,
    52,66
Hamlet Court School 71
Hamlet Estate 35
Hamlet House 68
Hamlet Lodge 68,69
Happy Valley *27,28*
Hardwick, John 18
Heygate, William 63
Hillborough Road 50
Hobleythick Lane 49
Holland, John 12
Holland Road 52
Hotel Mitre 71
Ingram, Mr 36
Inverness Avenue 35
Isolation Hospital 57
Iveagh, Lord 58
Jarvis, Peter 18
Jennings' 66
Kenilworth Gardens 52
Kernahan, Coulson 68
King's Cinema 4

King's Hall 4
Kings Road 58
Knight's 66
Lacell, John 12
Lazarus & Co 12
Legg, Richard 18
Leigh Road 54
Leigh Road Theatre 4
Lindisfarne College 71,*72*
Little Groomes 69
London Road 2,4,64
Manor Road 35
Marine Gardens 23
Mascot Cinema 2,*10*
Mason, George 54
Meteor Road 35
Meteor incident 18
Methodist Church 12
Metropole Cinema 6
Miles, Bernard 46
Mill Farm 18
Milton Church 4
Milton Road 6,34,50,66 ,71
Milton Hall 8,16
Milton Hall School 74
Milton Hamlet 6
Milton House 68
Milton Shore 16

Moat Field 54
Morice, Morice 69
Morrison family 69
Mountdale Gardens 52
Mower, - 14
Murdoch family 16
Nazareth House 9,10
Neave, A 38
Nelson Road 38
Newlands Road 50
Nolan, Frederick 45,46
North Clifton Estate 35
North Road 50,71
North Street 47
Northville Drive 48
Occupation Road 52
Old Oak 48
Osnaburgh Gardens 48
Outing, Joseph 21
Overcliff Hotel 29,31
Oysters 21
Palace Theatre 3,4,36
Palmeira Arches 25
Palmeira Towers 31
Palmerston Road 35
Park Estate 34
Park Road 12
Park Street 34

Piccadilly Road 52
Piccadilly Steps 52
Plough Corner 3
Pollard, Waide 66
Preston Road 68
Prince Avenue 48
Prittle Brook 37
Prittlewell 6,16,45
Prittlewell Chase 50
Prittlewell Pest House 56,57
Pulter family 16
Queen's Hotel 31,32
Quyk, John 38
Ramuz, Frederick 36,44
Ramuz Drive 18,37,58
Recko House 25
Reed family 16
Rich, Richard 8,38
Ridgeway 54
Roots Hall 2
Rossi, Pietro 25
St Bernard's High School 70,71
St Helen's Church 71
St Helen's Road 69
St Mary's, Prittlewell 35
St Mary's Convent 71
St Ursula's 58
St Vincent's Road 69

Salisbury Road 18,50
Sallendines Lane 52
Salomons, David 63
San Remo Parade 44
Sands, Edwin 14
Satanita Road 35
Scott family 16
Scratton, Daniel 8,12,21, 38,46
Scratton, John B 8
Scratton, Robert 66
Seaforth Road 35
Seymour Road 58
Shepherd's Cottage 65,66
Shorefield House 43,44,68
Shorefield Road 52
Snell's Farm 69
Somerset Gardens Estate 35
Southbourne Drive 52
Southchurch 4
Southend General Hospital 58
Southend Park 35
Springfield Drive 59
Station Road 55
Stockwell's 64
Summercourt Road 50
Swete, Robert 54
Swimming Bath 22,25
Thompson's Farm 69

Townsend, Mr 36
Treecot Drive 52
Tyrrell, Anthony 16
Unthank, Josias 47
Valkyrie Road 35,64,71
Victoria Avenue 47,74
Victoria Hospital 58
Vincent's Farm 69
Warrior Square 58
Washers 69
West Cliff Hotel 30,31
West Cliff Park Estate 35
West Road 17
Westborough Road 35
Westborough School 73
Westcliff High School 52,74
Westcliff Hospital 58
Westcliff Leisure Centre 25
Westcliff Station 62,63
Westward Ho! Hotel 31,33
White Hall 57
Whitefriars Crescent 35
Wickford Road 66
Wixley's 66
Wonnacott, J 10
Wood, George 44
Wood, Matthew 63